Screw It, Let's Do It

Lessons in Life

Screw It, Let's Do It

Lessons in Life

Richard Branson

13

First published in 2006 by Virgin Books,
an imprint of Ebury Publishing

A Random House Group Company

Copyright © Richard Branson 2006

The Random House Group Limited Reg. No. 954009

Addresses for companies within the Random House Group can be
found at www.randomhouse.co.uk

A CIP catalogue record for this book
is available from the British Library

Penguin Random House is committed to a sustainable future for
our business, our readers and our planet. This book is made from
Forest Stewardship Council® certified paper.

Printed and bound in Great Britain by Clays Ltd, St Ives plc

ISBN 9780753511671

CONTENTS

INTRODUCTION

THE PRESS CALL ME and my partners at Virgin 'Mavericks in Paradise'. There's no doubt that we tend to do things in a less stuffy way than most businesses – and I have ended up with two tropical islands to have fun on – so it must be true. And for me it works. I work hard and I play hard.

Though I have never followed the rules at every step, I have learned many lessons along the way. My lessons in life started at home when I was young. They carried on at school and in business from as early as my teens when I ran *Student* magazine. I am still learning and hope I never stop. These lessons have done me good throughout my life. I have written them down and I hope that you will find something in these pages that might inspire you.

I believe in goals. It's never a bad thing to have a dream, but I'm practical about it. I don't sit daydreaming about things that are impossible. I set goals and then work out how to achieve them. Anything I want to do in life I want to do well and not half-heartedly. At school, I found reading and writing hard. Back then, dyslexia wasn't understood and my teachers just thought I was lazy. So I taught myself to learn things by heart. Now I have a very good memory and it has become one of my best tools in business.

When I was starting out in life, things were more certain than they are these days. You had a career lined up, often the same one your father followed. Most mothers stayed at home. Today nothing is sure, and life is one long struggle. People have to make choices if they are to get anywhere. The best lesson I learned was to *just do it*. It doesn't matter what it is, or how hard it might seem, as the ancient Greek, Plato, said, 'The beginning is the most important part of any work.'

A journey of a thousand miles starts with that first step. If you look ahead to the end, and all the weary miles between, with all the dangers you might face, you might never take that first step. And whatever it is you want to achieve in life, if you don't make the effort, you won't reach your goal. So take that first step. There will be many challenges. You might get knocked back – but in the end, you will make it. Good luck!

Richard Branson

1. JUST DO IT!

Believe It Can Be Done
Have Goals
Live Life to the Full
Never Give Up
Prepare Well
Have Faith in Yourself
Help Each Other

THE STAFF AT VIRGIN have a name for me. It is 'Dr Yes'. They call me this because I won't say no. I find more reasons to do things than not to do them. My motto really is: 'Screw it – let's do it!'

I will never say, 'I can't do this because I don't know how to.' I will give it a go. I won't let silly rules stop me. I will find a legal way around them. I tell my staff, 'If you want to do it, just do it.' That way we all benefit. The staff's work and ideas are valued and Virgin gains from their input and drive.

I don't believe that that little word *'can't'* should stop you. If you don't have the right experience to reach your goal, look for another way in. If you want to fly, get down to the airfield at the age of sixteen and make the tea. Keep your eyes open. Look and learn. You don't have to go to art school to be a fashion designer. Join a fashion company and push a broom. Work your way up.

My mum, Eve, is a perfect example of this. During the war, she wanted to be a pilot. She went to Heston airfield and asked for a job. She was told only men could be pilots. Mum was very pretty and had been a dancer on stage. She didn't *look* like a man. That didn't stop her. She wore a leather flying jacket and hid her blonde hair under a leather helmet. She talked with a deep voice. And she got the job she wanted. She learned how to glide and began to teach the new pilots. These were the young men who flew fighter planes in the Battle of Britain.

After the war, she wanted to be an air hostess. Back then, they had to speak Spanish and be trained as nurses, but Mum chatted up the night porter at the airline and he secretly put her name on the list. Soon, she was an air hostess. She still couldn't speak Spanish and she wasn't a nurse. But she had used her wits. She wouldn't say no. She just did it.

Mum wasn't the only person in our family who said, 'Let's do it!'

The famous explorer, Captain Robert Scott, was my grandad's cousin. He was a man of great courage. He made two trips to the Antarctic. His goal was to be the first man to the South Pole. People said it couldn't be done. He said, 'I can do it.' And he nearly did it. He reached the South Pole, but he was second. Roald Amundsen got there first. It was a great blow for Scott. He died on the return journey. When people say there are no prizes for being second, I think of him. He is famous for being second to the South Pole. He also made the first balloon flight over Antarctica, but people don't remember that.

I started *Student* magazine when I was fifteen years old and still at school. Some people said I couldn't do it. They said I was too young and had no experience. But I wanted to prove them wrong and I believed it could be done. I did my sums with care. I worked out how much the paper and print bill would be. Then I worked out the income from sales and from selling advertising space.

Mum gave me four pounds for stamps. My school friend, Jonny Gems, and I spent almost two years writing hundreds of letters trying to sell space. I also tried to get interviews with famous people. Writing those letters and waiting for the replies was more fun than Latin lessons. It gave me a huge buzz when we got our first cheque for advertising space. It was £250, a huge amount. My belief had paid off.

I wasn't very good at passing exams at school. I knew I would do better on my own in the world. My parents let me make that choice. They were behind me, whatever I did. So I left school when I was sixteen to work full time on *Student*. Jonny and I camped out in the basement of his parents' London house. It was great to be young and free and in London. We drank beer, had girlfriends and listened to loud music. We were like students who didn't have to study. We worked just as hard, though. I got some first-rate interviews, with John Lennon, Mick Jagger, Vanessa Redgrave and Dudley Moore. We had more famous names than some of the top magazines. Famous people started dropping by. Life in the basement was glorious chaos. It was like a non-stop party.

But we had a serious side as well. We sent our own people out to cover the big issues of the day, like the war in Vietnam and the famine in Biafra. We felt we were changing things. What we did was important as well as fun. We were a close-knit team. Even my family helped to sell magazines. Mum took a big bundle to the park and sold them there. Each time a chance came, we grabbed it.

We branched out by being the first people to sell cut-price records by mail order – the first advert went in the last edition of *Student*. When a postal strike stopped us, we looked for another way. We wouldn't give in. Our goal was to open record shops but we didn't have enough money. So we talked a man who owned a shoe shop into letting us use his spare space. We worked hard to promote the opening. We made the store a 'cool' place for students to go. And one store led to a second and a third. Soon, we had stores in almost every big town – and I was still under twenty years old. Cash was pouring in fast. But I didn't sit back. We had reached that target but I still had more goals.

*

One of my big goals in life is that, like Captain Scott, I have always wanted to live life to the full. So, in 1984, when I was asked to sponsor a powerboat to win the Blue Riband for Britain, I agreed at once. The Blue Riband is a prize for the fastest ocean crossing from America to Ireland. I said I'd join the crew and trained hard. There was only one slight hitch. Joan and I were due to have a baby and I had promised her that I would be there for the birth. Then we were told that the weather was just right for the record attempt. I would let down the team if I didn't go.

I asked Joan, 'What shall I do?'

'Just do it – go,' she said. 'The baby's not due for two weeks. You'll be back before then.'

We set off, crashing across the waves in *Virgin Atlantic Challenger*. At the end of the first day, I got the news that my son, Sam had been born. We cracked open the champagne and kept going. The prize for the fastest crossing ever was within our grasp until we hit a huge storm off Ireland. Sixty miles from the end, we were hit by a giant wave. The hull split and we sank.

'Mayday! Mayday! Mayday!'

We were in the sea in the middle of a storm, in a life raft. A boat on its way to America saved us. We had failed in our first attempt to win the Blue Riband, but we didn't give in. Six years later, I was back with *Virgin Atlantic Challenger II*. Things were going well until we found that sea water was getting into our fuel tanks. The engines stopped. We spent hours cleaning the tanks and trying to start the engines. It seemed hopeless. The others at last said we had to give up. They said it was over. But I knew it was our last try. If we didn't do it now, we would never do it. I had to persuade them not to give in. I said, 'Come on, we've got to do it. Let's try.'

We were all done in. Our eyeballs were red and tired. We were all seasick. We hated the boat. We hated the sea. We wanted to sleep for a week.

'We've got to go on,' I yelled.

'All right,' they agreed. 'We'll give it one last shot.'

Somehow we started the engines and got going again. It seemed hopeless. We were so far behind that there seemed little point in trying. But we kept going. We made up time. In the end we beat the record by just two hours and nine minutes – but we did it. The lesson I learned from that and that I live by is to keep trying and to never give up.

The day after we had won the Blue Riband, a Swede named Per Lindstrand asked me to cross the Atlantic again – in a hot-air balloon.

I thought of my old hero, Captain Scott. He had flown in a balloon over the South Pole. I had never been in a balloon before. No one had ever flown that far in a balloon before. It was mad. It was too risky. By then, my companies were dealing in hundreds of millions of pounds. What would happen if I died?

There were many problems. But I can't resist a challenge and the chance to try something new. I said, 'Screw it – let's do it!'

But first, I asked Per, 'Do you have any children?'

'Yes,' he said. 'I've got two.'

That was good enough for me – if he would take the challenge, so would I. I shook his hand and said I would join him.

I always tell people that if they want to do anything well, they must plan and prepare. So I went to Spain with Per and learned to fly in a balloon. I didn't know it then, but those lessons saved my life.

One of the things I learnt was that each hot-air balloon carries fuel, which is burnt to heat the air in the balloon. Hot air rises and so does the balloon. When the fuel is not burnt, the air cools and the balloon drops lower in the sky. When flying a hot-air balloon, the pilot must heat or cool the air so that the balloon is at the right level to catch the wind going in the direction the balloon needs to go.

The winds and the jet stream blow from America to Europe. We left from America and 29 hours later, we were over Ireland. We were the first to cross the Atlantic in a hot-air balloon. There was only one problem – how to land. We had some full fuel tanks left and it was too dangerous to land with them. We might crash and burn. We chose to come down low and drop the tanks in a field. We reduced the flame in the balloon and came down low. We cut the tanks free. But then we were too light. We bounced across a field and shot up into the sky, out of control.

'Let's come down on the beach, where we won't hurt people,' Per said.

We flew into thick fog and missed the beach. The sea looked very black and stormy. If we landed in it with the balloon, we could drown. I struggled into my life jacket. Suddenly, from around 56 feet up, Per jumped into the icy sea. Without his weight, the balloon shot up too high for me to jump. I was on my own.

I floated higher and higher into the clouds. The winds took me north, towards Scotland. I was alone, flying in the biggest balloon ever built. I had about an hour of fuel left. When it went, I would fall into the sea. I tried the radio. It was dead. I didn't know what to do. I could jump out in my parachute or stay put. I wrote in my notebook, 'Joan, Holly, Sam, I love you.'

'While I'm alive, I can still do something,' I said to myself. 'Something will turn up.' Something did. As the balloon drifted down towards the grey sea, I came out of the clouds and saw a helicopter. It was searching for me! I waved and the crew waved back. I was safe.

Close to the waves, I jumped into the sea, away from the balloon. Without my weight, it flew up and out of sight. The helicopter fished me out of the icy water. I asked about Per, but they had thought he was with me. He had been in the sea for hours. We had to find him quickly. I told them where he would be and he was rescued just before he froze to death.

The whole trip was an amazing experience. I learned many lessons: not just if you want to do something, just do it, but also to prepare well, have faith in yourself, help each other, never give up.

All of these lessons can be used in life. You don't have to run a big business, fly in a balloon, or break records in a boat to learn from and use the lessons I learned. Your goal can be small. *Student* magazine was very small at first. I sold space in it from a payphone at school because I believed I could and would do it. If something is what you really want to do, just do it. Whatever your goal is you will never succeed unless you let go of your fears and fly.

2. HAVE FUN!

Have Fun, Work Hard and Money Will Come
Don't Waste Time – Grab Your Chances
Have a Positive Outlook on Life
When it's Not Fun, Move On

I DON'T DENY THAT I have done well and had success. It has even been said that I turn what I touch into gold. People ask me what my secret is. How do I make money? What they really want to know is – *how can* they *make money?* Everyone wants to be a millionaire.

I always tell them the same thing. I have no secret. There are no rules to follow in business. I just work hard and, as I always have done, believe I can do it. Most of all, though, I try to have fun.

When I was about to go around the world in a hot-air balloon in 1997 I knew that it was very risky. I might not return. Before I left, I wrote a letter to my children, Sam and Holly. In it, I said, 'Live life to the full. Enjoy every minute of it. Love and look after Mum.'

Those words sum up what I believe in. Don't waste time. Have fun. Love your family.

Notice that making money isn't in that list.

I didn't set out to be rich. The fun and the challenge in life were what I wanted – and still do. I don't deny that money is important. We are not cavemen and women. We can't live just on roots and berries. We live in an era when we must have some money to survive. I once said I only need one breakfast, one lunch and one dinner a day. And I still live by those words. I never went into business to make money – but I have found that, if I have fun, the money will come. I often ask myself, is my work fun and does it make me happy? I believe that the answer to that matters more than fame or fortune. If something stops being fun, I ask *why?* If I can't fix it, I stop doing it.

You might ask, how do I know that fun will lead to money? Of course it doesn't always happen. I have had my downs as well as ups. But on the whole I have been very lucky. For

13

almost as long as I can remember, I've had fun and I've made money.

My very first business lessons were not a success, but I learned from them. My first money-making scheme was when I was about nine years old. One Easter I came up with a great plan. I would grow Christmas trees. I asked my best friend, Nik Powell, to help me plant 400 seeds in our field at home. We worked hard but also enjoyed ourselves. We enjoyed messing about on the farm. All we had to do was wait for the seeds to turn into Christmas trees. It would take eighteen months. The first thing I had to learn was how to use figures. I was not good at sums at school. On paper, they made no sense. But as I planned our Christmas tree business, I used *real* sums that did make sense. The bag of seeds cost just £5 and we would sell each tree for £2. We would make £795, which was worth waiting for. Even at an early age I planned long term and learned to wait for reward.

My second lesson was that money doesn't grow on trees! Sadly, rabbits ate all the seedlings. We got some revenge, though. I'm sorry to say we had fun shooting the rabbits.

We sold them for a shilling each to the local butcher. Overall, we did make a small profit and all our friends had rabbit pie. We all gained something.

You never know what you'll find on a sunny beach . . . On holiday, I found my very own desert island and an airline. In 1976 I was working hard building up Virgin Music. Mike Oldfield had already been our first big success with *Tubular Bells* in 1973. We also signed up the Sex Pistols so things were on the up. We were very busy but we all also had a great deal of fun. People said things like 'Branson's a lucky devil' to come across a huge hit like *Tubular Bells*. Yes, it was a lucky break, but we grabbed it. It had been taken to every other record company. They had turned it down. But we heard it and believed in it. We knew it could happen. Making it work was hard for a bunch of kids like us, though. We had to find the money. We had to push it to the top. We had to think differently. We asked John Peel to play the entire album on his show and he did. It had never been done before. And it worked. Sales took off.

RICHARD BRANSON

Mike Oldfield was too shy to promote the album. *We found an answer.* We made a video and showed it on TV. Our big breakthrough was when we got it used as the soundtrack of *The Exorcist.* Sales were massive. We were a success, but we never stopped looking for new sounds and new talent.

By the end of 1977 I needed a break. My girlfriend, Joan, and I had split up. I was sad but I like to make the best of things. I always like to get away from London in the winter. Music, sun and sea make me feel good. The distance from London gives me the space and freedom to think and plan out fresh ideas.

I went to Jamaica. It was part holiday, part work. I swam in a warm sea. I sat on the beach. I listened to some great reggae bands. Then we heard a new kind of music. It was made by local DJs and radio jocks, who were known as 'toasters'. It was a kind of early rap, so I was in at the start of something big. Jamaican musicians won't take cheques so I signed up almost twenty reggae bands and some toasters from a case filled with cash. We went on to sell lots of records with them. It was a perfect example of my motto – have fun and the money will come.

I was still in Jamaica when Joan phoned me out of the blue. 'Can you meet me in New York?' she said. We had a happy time in New York City, but the phone didn't stop ringing. We longed to escape and spend some time alone. Someone asked me if I had named Virgin after the Virgin Islands. The answer was no. We had named the company Virgin because we were virgins in business. But I had never been to the Virgin Islands. And they sounded like the perfect romantic place for Joan and me.

I had spent all our cash on signing up bands in Jamaica. But I had heard that if you were looking for a house on an island, you would get a grand tour, free of charge. I phoned an estate agent in the British Virgin Islands. I said I owned a record company and wanted to buy an island to build a studio on it.

'Please come as our guests. We have lots of lovely islands for sale. We'll show you around.'

Joan and I flew to the British Virgin Islands. We were treated like royalty. A big car met us at the airport and took us to a villa. It was like being in paradise. The next day a helicopter was waiting to take us on a tour. We skimmed over green palm trees and a blue sea. We landed on

17

one lovely island after the other. We toured fantastic private estates and had a great time. We spun our free holiday out as long as we could, but at last we were running out of islands for sale.

We asked the agent if he had something that we hadn't seen.

'Yes, there's one, a real little jewel,' he said. 'It's miles from anywhere and it's quite unspoiled. Its name is Necker.' He said an English lord owned it, a man who had never been there.

An island that was miles from anywhere sounded good on two counts. The first was it was a nice long flight with plenty of scenery for us to enjoy. The second was we really did like the sound of it. Unspoiled meant that it had not been built on. Perhaps it would be cheap.

At first, island hopping was a game. We didn't mean to buy an island. I didn't think I could afford one. But now I was excited. I wanted to own our own place in paradise. *I had another goal.*

We flew over a blue sea and could see pale sand at the bottom. We landed on a white sandy beach. There was a green hill in the middle, and we climbed up it. The view from the top was worth the effort. We could see in every direction. The island was inside a coral reef. The white beach ran almost all the way around. The agent told us that turtles laid their eggs on the beach. The sea was so clear we could see a giant ray swimming along. In the middle of the island were two small lakes. There was a lush, tropical forest. A flock of black parrots flew overhead. There were no big villas. It was a real desert island. Standing there, gazing out to sea, I was king of all I saw. I fell in love with Necker on the spot.

The agent warned us that there was no fresh water on the island. If we bought it, we would have to make it from the sea.

'Good,' I thought. 'They can't be asking a lot for a desert island with no water and no house.' I asked him the price.

'Three million pounds,' he said.

It was far beyond my reach. 'I can offer £150,000,' I replied.

I was offering less than five per cent of the asking price! I was serious but the agent wasn't amused. 'The price is three million pounds,' he repeated.

'Final offer. I can go to £200,000,' I said.

We walked back down that hill and got into the helicopter. We flew back to the villa. Our bags were waiting outside. We had been thrown out. We spent the night in a bed and breakfast in the village and left the next day.

We spent the rest of our holiday on another island. Our plan was to travel on to Puerto Rico – but when we got to the airport, the flight was cancelled. People were roaming about, looking lost. No one was doing anything. So I did – someone had to. I chartered a plane for $2,000. I divided that by the number of people. It came to $39 a head. I borrowed a blackboard and wrote on it: VIRGIN AIRWAYS. $39 SINGLE FLIGHT TO PUERTO RICO.

The idea for Virgin Airways was born, right in the middle of a holiday, although the actual airline only properly took off when I was sent a business idea. I had never chartered a plane before, but, as with *Tubular Bells* and the Jamaican toasters, I saw and grabbed the chance. And look at Virgin Atlantic today! We fly to 30 places around the world. We have Virgin Blue in Australia, Virgin Express in Europe and Virgin Nigeria. We are planning

Virgin America. And we've even gone further –
Virgin Galactic will offer flights into space. No
one else is doing that. It's a bold move. We are
ahead of everyone. In 21 years we have gone
from renting a plane to space travel.

Back in London with Joan after our holiday, I
still had my goal to buy Necker Island. I did
some research. I found that the owner of Necker
was not rich, which is why he had never
developed the island. I also found that he
wanted to sell in a hurry so he could raise
£200,000 to build a house in London. It was the
same sum I had offered the agent. It seemed
that my offer was meant to be!

The only problem was, I didn't have
£200,000, so I was going to have to borrow it
from someone. I offered £175,000, which I
didn't have either. It was turned down. I left it
at that and got on with work. Three months
later, I got a call to say the island was mine if I
offered £180,000. I was told that, as part of the
deal, I had to build a house and a plant to take
the salt out of the sea water so that we could use
it within five years. This would cost a lot. But I
was positive I could find the money somewhere
to do it and I agreed to the terms.

21

Now all I had to do was find the money to buy the island of my dreams. It seemed out of reach, but I vowed to reach my goal. I promised myself that I would make enough money to pay for the island, which I did, by taking on loans from the bank and by borrowing from my friends and family. So, while it doesn't have to be buying an island, this is why I can say, have fun and the money will come and in turn so will your goals.

Today, Necker is a lovely place, where all my friends and family gather together to relax and play. The last episode of my TV series, *The Rebel Billionaire* was filmed there. The camera filmed from the terrace. It showed our wonderful view of the sea, the white sandy beach and the palm trees. It was the same view that Joan and I saw from the top of that green hill all those years ago. I signed up bands on Jamaica and ended up with an airline and an island. It wasn't always easy. But when you have goals and a positive outlook on life, you have something to aim for. Hard work and fun is what life is all about.

As soon as something stops being fun, I think it's time to move on. Life is too short to be unhappy. Waking up stressed and miserable is not a good way to live. I found this out years ago in my working relationship with my oldest friend, Nik Powell.

Nik was with me from the very start of Virgin. I was the ideas person and Nik kept the books in order and handled the money. His main job was to run the Virgin record stores. They did very well. When we started the airline, we wanted it to be the best. We sank millions of pounds into it. Our main rivals, British Airways, tried to stop us. As the war between us heated up, we needed more and more money. It seemed an endless pit. Virgin Music was wealthy but the airline was eating up the cash. Nik didn't enjoy taking such huge risks. That was when we both knew it was time for him to move on. I bought his shares in Virgin from him.

Nik's first love had always been films. He used his profit from Virgin to start Palace Pictures. He made great films, like *The Company of Wolves*, *Mona Lisa* and *The Crying Game*, which won an Oscar. He is still in the film business, still having fun and we are still friends. After a struggle, the airline finally went into profit. If Nik had stayed with Virgin he might have made more money, but he would not have been happy. If we had gone on working together even after the fun had gone, we might not have stayed friends. He made the right choice. This is why I say, never just try to make money. Long-term success will never come if profit is the only aim.

I have been lucky. Virgin now has the luxury of a great deal of money behind it. People say I should relax. I could retire. I ask, 'What would I do?'

They say, 'Paint watercolours. Play golf. Have fun.'

But I am already having fun. My work is fun. Fun is at the core of the way I do business. It has been the key to it all from the start. I see no reason to change it.

Not all of us have the money to start up a business, or the luck, or the chances aren't there. Sometimes, you are just glad to have a job – any job. So you grab the job in the factory or the store or the call centre. You might hate it, but you try to make the best of things. But is that fun? I would say do you really have to stay stuck in a rut? Is that job you hate really your only option? Whoever you are, you have other choices. Look around. See what else you can do.

The internet has opened many new doors. A friend of mine wanted to hire a van. So he looked on the net and soon had twenty offers of a van with a working driver. There are work and trading chances on the web – it has changed the lives of people with ideas and energy. Even those with little experience can create a successful internet mail-order business. Wilf and Kathy started Chillis Galore by making chilli jelly to give away to their friends in their kitchen in Norfolk fifteen years ago. They progressed to selling at fairs and the response from chilli lovers everywhere led them to go online. Today, they make and sell a big range of unusual jellies and relishes. All their chillis are still grown in two greenhouses in the back garden. Prince Charles sells his organic food online. And there's even a mail order Christmas tree business – Christmas Tree Land – which started out as a small roadside stall. Today, they sell anything festive – from baubles to bells. (So I was right, back when I was eight years old. If the rabbits had behaved, I could have been a Christmas tree king!)

Even without the internet anyone can start up a new business from home. You can wash windows, take in ironing or walk dogs. You can be an artist or a writer. You can be a gardener. You can make and sell dolls' houses. Anita Roddick made skin cream in her kitchen. Now the Body Shop is a global empire. You can make salad dressing in your garage like Paul Newman. With him it started as a hobby. Now it's a big company. (He gives all the profits to charity. So far, he has given away more than $150 million – not bad for a hobby.) Granted, Paul Newman didn't have to worry about funding. But there are dozens of things you can do from home to make money. It could be more fun and lead to a new career you really enjoy.

If you do still have to work for a boss at a job you don't like, as almost everyone does at some point, don't moan about it. Have a positive outlook on life and just get on with it. Work hard and earn your pay. Enjoy the people you come into contact with through your job. And if you are still unhappy, make it instead your goal to divide your private life from your work life. Have fun in your own time, you will feel happier and you'll enjoy your life and your job more.

3. BE BOLD

Calculate the Risks and Take Them
Believe in Yourself
Chase Your Dreams and Goals
Have No Regrets
Be Bold
Keep Your Word

IN 2004 I MADE a TV series, *The Rebel Billionaire*. The final episode had a twist at the end. I offered the prizewinner, Shawn Nelson, a cheque for one million dollars – but there was a catch. He could take the cheque or toss a coin for an even bigger mystery prize. If he lost the toss, he would lose it all. I held out the cheque. He took it and saw the long line of zeros. Then I took it back and put it in my hip pocket. I held out a silver coin.

'Which one will it be?' I said. 'The coin or the cheque?'

Life is full of hard choices. Which one would he go for?

Shawn looked shaken. It was a huge gamble. All or nothing. He asked me, 'What would you do, Richard?'

'It's up to you,' I said. I could have told him, 'I take risks, but they are calculated risks. I weigh up the odds in everything I do.' Instead, I said nothing. He had to make up his own mind.

Shawn walked back and forth, trying to decide. It was tempting to gamble. It would make him look cool. Also, the unknown prize might be amazing. At last, he said he couldn't risk losing that much money on the toss of a coin. He owned a small company. He could use the money wisely to help his business grow. It could change his life for the better. It would also help the people who worked for him and believed in him.

'I'll take the cheque,' he said.

I was pleased. 'If you had gone for the coin toss, I would have lost all respect for you,' I said.

He made the right choice and didn't gamble on something that he couldn't control. He got the million dollars *and* the mystery prize. The big prize was to be president of Virgin for three months. Virgin has 200 companies so Shawn would learn a lot. It was a golden chance.

I am always looking for that certain something in people like Shawn that makes them different to other people. People who work at Virgin are special. They aren't sheep. They think for themselves. They have good ideas and I listen to them. What is the point of hiring bright people if you don't use their talent?

One of the things I try to do at Virgin is make people think about themselves and see themselves more positively. I firmly believe that anything is possible. I tell them, 'Believe in yourself. You can do it.'

I also say, 'Be bold but don't gamble.'

I get sent thousands of ideas each week – they are people's goals and dreams. There are too many for me to look at. My staff read them first and weed them out. I look at the best ones.

One plan I was offered ended in disaster. I was young. My urge to try anything almost killed me. Sadly, it killed the inventor.

A man called Richard Ellis sent me a photo of his 'flying machine'. It had a three-wheeled bike beneath two large wings. It was powered by a small outboard engine. There were rotors above the pilot's head. The photo showed a man soaring above the treetops. I was curious and I invited him to show me how it worked.

When he came, we went to the local airfield with Joan and some friends. He took his machine to a landing strip. You had to pedal like mad to get speed up. Then the engine would cut in and start the rotors. He said I would be the second person to try it. But he didn't want me to fly.

'You need to get used to it first,' he said.

It looked like fun. I sat on the machine. He gave me a cable with a rubber switch at the end, which went in my mouth. I had to bite on the switch to make the engine cut out. I would stop at the end of the runway before I took off.

'OK! Go!' Ellis shouted.

I put the cable in my mouth and set off down the runway. I pedalled like hell. The engine kicked in. I went faster and faster. When it seemed fast enough, I bit into the switch to stop. Nothing happened. I went even faster. I bit harder. Nothing. I reached thirty miles an hour. I could see Joan looking at me at the end of the runway as I got closer. Suddenly, I rose into the air. The flying machine took off, with me hanging on. I was flying.

I soared over some trees. I rose higher. When I was at one hundred feet, I knew I had to stop it somehow. I tugged at wires and pulled them out. I burned my hands on the hot engine but at last the engine cut out and I spun down to the ground. At the very last moment, a small gust of wind flipped the machine over. A wing took the impact. I fell out onto the grass. I was safe but shocked.

A week later, Ellis took off in the flying machine. It crashed to earth. He died on impact.

His death was sad, but people with vision do die. Mountain climbers fall, and test pilots crash. As a child, I knew the war hero, Douglas Bader. He was a friend of my Aunt Clare's. He lost his legs in a flying accident. He learned to walk and he also flew again. You can take care and try to avoid the risks, but you can't protect yourself all the time. I am sure that luck plays a very large part. It's easy to give up when things are hard but I believe we have to keep chasing our dreams and our goals, as these exciting

31

people did. And once we decide to do something, we should never look back, never regret it.

One decision I didn't regret was a proposal from a young American lawyer. In 1984 he wanted me to invest in a new airline that would fly across the Atlantic. Even before I read his plan I had wanted to do it. Freddie Laker, a childhood hero of mine, ran Skytrain, a cut-price airline between England and America. He was a big man with bold ideas. He was David to the Goliath of the big airlines. He wanted to make air travel cheap enough so that more people could afford it, but the airline had collapsed in 1982. With Freddie and my plane chartering to get to Puerto Rico in mind, I read the proposal. It would cost a great deal of money and I told myself, 'Don't be tempted. Don't even think about it.'

But I was tempted. The idea grabbed me. It was exciting.

I can make up my mind about people and ideas in sixty seconds. I rely more on gut instinct than thick reports. I knew within a minute that this was for me. It was a very bold step, but worth it. I decided to look into it. I had to work out in my own mind what the risks were.

There was already a popular airline that sold cheap fares across the Atlantic. It was called People Express. I tried to call them. It seemed everyone must have wanted to fly as their lines were busy. I tried all day but couldn't get through. I knew I could run an airline better than that. I spent a weekend thinking it over. By Sunday evening I had made up my mind. I would be bold. I would *just do it.*

On Monday, I called Boeing, the biggest American company that made planes. I asked how much it would cost to rent a jumbo jet for a year. They were surprised, but they listened to me. By the end of the call, we had worked out a good price. I felt I had done enough research. I met my partners in Virgin Music to discuss it.

They said I was crazy. I said that we could afford it. We had to be bold. 'I don't want us to sit on our money like misers. It's there to be used,' I said.

They still didn't look happy so I pressed on. I said that Virgin Music was making a lot of money. The money to start an airline was less than a third of a year's profits. It was a lot, but not too much. Even if we lost it all, we would survive. 'It's not too big a risk. And it'll be fun.'

They weren't happy with the word 'fun'. To them, business was serious. It is. But, to me, having fun matters more. I want to live life to the full. I want new goals to reach for. I decided to call the airline Virgin Atlantic.

I asked Sir Freddie Laker to lunch to talk about my new project. He was a great help. He had years of experience. Most of all, he knew the problems in starting a new airline. His airline had done well until the big airlines undercut him. They had the money to keep going. They could afford to make losses while they drove his new airline out. Freddie ran on a shoestring. He ran out of money and went bust. Over lunch, he told me how an airline worked. We discussed what I should look out for.

Freddie said, 'Look out for dirty tricks from British Airways. BA's dirty tricks ruined me. Don't let them ruin you. Complain as loudly as you can. My mistake was that I didn't complain.'

I don't like to complain. I don't cry over spilled milk. I just get on with things. But I made a mental note. 'Watch out for dirty tricks. Complain loudly.'

Freddie also advised, 'Don't make it a cheap, no-frills service. The big airlines can undercut you, like they did to me. Instead offer a better service than they do, at a good price. People want comfort. And don't forget the fun. People like to have fun. Good luck. Be ready for a great deal of stress.'

All of his advice was helpful when I had to talk to officials. Safety was a big concern. Making sure the airline was well funded was another. I worked out a cash-flow survival plan. I hired the right people. I got a good team. I stuck to it. I wouldn't take no for an answer. I found other ways around problems. And, believe me, there were endless problems.

BA did try dirty tricks against us. They tried to destroy us by ruining my name. Sir Freddie said, 'Sue the bastards!' and I took BA to court for libel – and won.

When Virgin Atlantic launched in 1984, not one person thought it would survive for more than a year. The bosses of the big American airline companies said I'd fail. Now they are all out of business. I'm still there.

I was bold, yes, but not foolish. I took a risk by starting up an airline. But the odds were good. They were not all or nothing, like they were with the winner of *The Rebel Billionaire*, and I had thought through how to manage the risks. Shawn Nelson could have won it all or lost it all on the spin of a coin. It took courage to refuse.

My next big venture was starting Virgin Trains in 1996. I got the idea when I was in Japan. I was there to look for a site to build a new Megastore. When we took the bullet train, I thought it was great. It was like being on a plane.

'Why can't trains be like this in the UK?' I thought. I jotted down some notes to remind me. It was fate. The next week the UK government said they would break up the old train system, British Rail, and let new businesses compete to run trains. I jumped in and said I was interested. The news hit the papers: VIRGIN TO GO INTO TRAINS. They said it was a bold move.

Again, as with the airline, some people said I would fail. It took five years but we did it. We produced the world's most advanced leaning train. It was a proud moment when my wife Joan named it *Virgin Lady*. At the time, it went too fast for the UK's old tracks. Once again, we were ahead of everyone. The TV news said we had made good on our promises.

One thing I always try to do is to keep my word. I set my goals and stick to them. Success is more than luck. You have to believe in yourself and make it happen. That way others also believe in you.

Sometimes, I get business offers that I turn down. I had the chance to invest in Ryanair, a good, no-frills airline. I turned it down. Ryanair is still going strong. I also turned down the chance to invest in Trivial Pursuit and a wind-up radio. All of them were good ideas. I turned down the chance to be a Lloyd's name. Lloyd's is the biggest insurance company in the world. They insure against huge losses like hurricanes and earthquakes. Turning them down, though, was a good choice. I could have lost a fortune.

Some you win and some you lose. Be glad when you win. Don't have regrets when you lose. Never look back. You can't change the past. I try to learn from it. We can't all run big airlines or trains. Many people have more modest goals. *But whatever your dream is, go for it.* Always beware if the risks are too random or too hard to predict, but remember, if you opt for a safe life, you will never know what it's like to win.

4. CHALLENGE YOURSELF

Aim High
Try New Things
Always Try
Challenge Yourself

EVERYONE NEEDS SOMETHING TO aim for. You can call it a challenge, or you can call it a goal. It is what makes us human. It was challenges that took us from being cavemen to reaching for the stars.

If you challenge yourself, you will grow. Your life will change. Your outlook will be positive. It's not always easy to reach your goals but that's no reason to stop. Never say die. Say to yourself, 'I can do it. I'll keep on trying until I win.'

For me, there are two types of challenge. One is to do the best I can at work. The other is to seek adventure. I try to do both. I try to stretch myself to the limit. I am driven. I love the

39

challenge of looking for new things and new ideas. To me, the search is fun.

My first big challenge came when I was four or five years old and we went to Devon for two weeks one summer. Dad's sisters and an uncle went with us. When we got there, I ran onto the beach and stared at the sea. I couldn't swim and Auntie Joyce bet me ten shillings that I couldn't learn to swim by the end of the holiday. I took the bet, sure I would win. Most days, the sea was rough and the waves were high, but I tried for hours. Day after day, I splashed along, with one foot on the bottom. I grew blue with cold and swallowed a lot of sea water, but still I couldn't swim.

'Never mind, Ricky,' Auntie Joyce said, kindly. 'There's always next year.'

I had lost the bet. I was sure she would forget about it the next year. As we set off home in the car, I gazed out of the window. How I wished I had learned to swim. I hated losing the bet. It was a hot day and in the 1950s the roads were very narrow. We weren't going very fast when I saw a river. We hadn't got home so we were still really on holiday. I knew it was my last chance to win.

'Stop the car!' I shouted. My parents knew about the bet and, though they obviously would not have done what I said when I was that age, I think my father knew what I wanted and how much it meant to me.

Dad drove off the road and parked. 'What's up?' he asked.

'Ricky wants to have another go at winning that ten shillings,' Mum said.

I jumped out of the car and stripped quickly, then ran across a field to the river. When I got to the bank, I felt scared. The river looked deep and fast, running over rocks. There was a muddy part where cows drank from. It was easy to reach the water from there. I turned my head and saw everyone standing, watching me.

Mum smiled and waved me on. 'You can do it, Ricky!' she called.

I walked through the mud and waded into the water. As soon as I got in the middle the current caught at me. I went under and choked. I came up, and was swept fast downstream. I took a deep breath and relaxed. I knew I could do it. I put one foot on a rock and pushed off. Soon, I was swimming. I swam in an awkward circle, but I'd won the bet. I heard the family

41

cheering on the bank. When I crawled out, I was done in, but very proud. I crawled through mud and stinging nettles to reach Auntie Joyce. She held up the ten shillings.

'Well done, Ricky!' she said.

'I knew you could do it,' Mum said. And so had I, and I was not going to give up until I had proved it.

One thing I couldn't do very well was read. I always found lessons hard at school because I was mildly dyslexic. I hated to admit defeat, but however hard I struggled, as with many other people, reading and writing were hard for me. For some reason this made me want to be a reporter, a job where reading and writing are always needed. When I found that my school had an essay contest, I entered. I don't know who was the most surprised when I won. I was the boy who was often caned for failing tests. But I had won an essay contest. I was thrilled.

When I told Mum, she said, 'I knew you could win, Ricky.' Mum is one of those people who never says 'can't'. She believes anything is possible if you try.

From then on, my school work improved. I

learned to focus on hard words and my spelling got better. I think this shows that you can achieve almost anything – but you have to make the effort. I didn't stop challenging myself. I went on from winning that essay prize to starting *Student* magazine. I think I wanted to prove that the boy who was caned for not being able to read or write very well could do it – and I did.

As I grew older, I faced bigger challenges. I seemed to run on high energy. I wanted adventure. Danger tempted me. I had already set a record for being the first to cross the Atlantic in a balloon with Per. Next, we decided to cross the Pacific Ocean, from Japan to the USA. It was a far more dangerous venture, across 8,000 miles of open sea. No one had ever done it before. I knew how risky it was because our rival had just died in an attempt. His balloon had torn and he landed in the freezing sea. It was so stormy, he couldn't be rescued in time, and he died from cold.

Joan didn't want me to go on this trip, and I must admit I was nervous. But I had promised to go and we were ready for the attempt. I couldn't withdraw, so I resigned myself to fate. My head said stop, but my heart said go. Whatever the danger, I wouldn't give in and I think Joan understood.

I knew it would be a strange trip. I was a team player, who always looked for the best in people. Per was a quiet loner, who always looked for the worst. I hoped we would balance each other out.

It was 1990, and, just before we left, I spent Christmas on a small island near Japan with my family and friends. It was very lovely and peaceful there. I watched men catching fish with tame birds. Their lives seemed calm and tranquil. I wondered what they would think of my constant rushing about. I only knew that challenges were what drove me onwards.

Our plan was to cross the ocean on one of the jet streams that circle the earth between 20,000 and 40,000 feet up. They travel as fast as a river in full flood. Below that, the winds are slower. Our problem was the height of our giant balloon from the top to the bottom of the capsule below. It was over 300 feet. As we broke through into the jet stream, the top half of the balloon and the bottom would travel at

44

different speeds. Anything could happen.

Inside the capsule we put on our parachutes and clipped ourselves to the life rafts so that if anything went wrong we did not waste valuable time doing that later. Then we fired the burners. As we rose, the top of the balloon hit the bottom of the jet stream. It was like hitting a glass ceiling. We burned more fuel to try to rise, but the winds were so strong they kept pushing us down. We burned even more fuel – and at last broke through. The top of the balloon was caught by the fast current and took off like a rocket. It was flying along at a crazy angle at 115 miles an hour. The capsule, with us inside it, was still going at 25mph. It felt like a thousand horses were dragging us apart. We feared the balloon would be torn in two, and the heavy capsule would hurtle thousands of feet down to the sea.

But, at the last moment, the capsule shot through the glass ceiling and the balloon righted itself.

'No one has ever done that before,' Per said.

We flew along at great speed, faster than we thought possible. Seven hours later it was time to lose the first empty fuel tank. It seemed safer to drop down out of the jet stream to do this. We cut off the burners and went down into a slower zone. At once, the capsule acted like a brake, but the balloon still hurtled along. We could see the angry grey sea 25,000 feet below us. I wondered if we would end up in it.

Per pressed the button to release the empty fuel tank. At once, the capsule lurched sideways. The floor tilted and I fell against Per. To our horror we found that two full tanks as well as the empty one had fallen off one side. They weighed a ton each. Not only were we lopsided and off balance, now we didn't have enough fuel to control our height and find the right wind pattern, so we couldn't reach the USA. Three tons lighter, the balloon soared upwards. We hit the jet stream so fast we shot through the glass ceiling like a bullet and kept on rising. Per let some air out of the balloon, but still we flew up and up.

We had been warned that the glass dome of our capsule would explode at 43,000 feet and our lungs and eyeballs would be sucked out of our bodies. At 41,000 feet we entered the unknown. We reached a frightening 42,500 feet. We had no idea what might happen. We were higher not only than any balloon had been, but than any aircraft had ever flown, except Concorde. At last we stopped rising. The balloon cooled and we started to fall fast. We didn't want to burn extra fuel, but we had to, to stop falling.

We couldn't come down in the sea because there was no one to rescue us. We would have to last for another thirty hours on almost no fuel. In order to reach land we had to fly faster than any balloon had ever flown before. That meant staying right in the centre of the jet stream, a space just a hundred yards wide. It seemed impossible.

The final straw was when we lost radio contact. We had been going for hours and Per was worn out. He lay down and fell into an instant, deep sleep. I was on my own. I don't believe in God, but that day it felt as if a guardian angel had entered the capsule and was helping us along. From the dials I saw that we had started to speed up, faster and faster. I thought I was dreaming and slapped my face to make sure I was awake. We went from 80 miles an hour, through to 180, then 200, then 240. This was unheard of. It seemed like a miracle.

I was so bone weary, I felt spaced out. When I saw strange, flickering lights in the glass dome, I thought they were spirits. I watched them as if in a dream, until I realised that burning lumps of gas were falling all around. It was minus 70 degrees outside. If a fireball hit the glass dome, it would explode.

'Per!' I yelled. 'Wake up! We're on fire!'

Per woke up fast. He knew at once what to do. 'Take her up to forty thousand feet where there's no oxygen,' he said. 'Then the fire will go out.'

At just under 43,000 feet the flames died and we started down again. But we had wasted precious fuel. Then the radio came back on. A voice said, 'War's broken out in the Gulf. The Americans are bombing Baghdad.' It seemed strange that while we were alone almost on the edge of space a war had just started on Earth.

Our ground crew told us our jet stream had turned. It would loop us back to Japan. We had to get into a lower jet stream at once, one that would take us to the Arctic. We dropped down to 30,000 feet and flew hour after hour at over 200 miles an hour in a lopsided capsule. We finally landed in a blizzard, on a frozen lake in the far north of Canada in a wild area 200 times the size of Britain. We were so far off the beaten track it took eight hours to be rescued. By then we both had frostbite.

'Next time, we'll fly around the world,' Per said.

I laughed, but I knew I couldn't turn down a challenge. We made the attempt a couple of years later, but someone beat us to it. Now I am planning space travel as my next big thing, with Virgin Galactic.

Just before we had left to cross the Pacific, my daughter, Holly, sent me a fax. She wrote, 'I hope you don't land in the water and have a bad landing. I hope you have a good landing and land on dry land.'

It seemed a perfect metaphor for my life. I have been lucky. So far, I have nearly always landed on dry land. I think the writer and mountain climber James Ullman summed it all up when he said something like, 'Challenge is the core and mainspring of all human action. If there's an ocean, we cross it. If there's a disease, we cure it. If there's a wrong, we right it. If there's a record, we break it. And if there's a mountain, we climb it.' I totally agree and believe we should all continue to challenge ourselves.

5. STAND ON YOUR OWN FEET

Rely on Yourself
Chase Your Dreams but Live in the
   Real World
Work Together

'IF YOU WANT MILK, don't sit on a stool in the middle of a field in the hope that the cow will back up to you.' This old saying could have been one of my mother's quotes. She would have added, 'Go on, Ricky. Don't just sit around. Catch the cow.'

An old recipe for rabbit pie said, 'First, catch the rabbit.' Note that it didn't say, 'First, buy the rabbit, or sit on your bottom until someone gives it to you.'

Lessons like this, taught to me by Mum from when I was a toddler, are what have made me stand on my own two feet. I was trained to think for myself and get things done. It's what the British as a nation used to believe in, but there are some kids today who seem to want everything handed to them on a plate. Perhaps if more parents were like mine were, we would be a nation of go-getters – as we used to be.

When I was four years old, Mum stopped the car a few miles from our house and told me to find my own way home across the fields. She made it a game, one I was happy to play. It was an early challenge. As I grew older, these lessons grew harder. Early one winter morning, Mum shook me awake and told me to get dressed. It was dark and cold, but I crawled out of bed. I was given a packed lunch and an apple. 'I'm sure you will find some water along the way,' Mum said, as she waved me off on a fifty-mile bike ride to the south coast. It was still dark when I set off on my own. I spent the night with a relative and returned home the next day. When I walked into the kitchen at home, I felt very proud. I was sure I would be greeted by cheers. Instead, Mum said, 'Well done, Ricky. Was that fun? Now run along, the vicar wants you to chop some logs for him.'

To some people this might sound harsh. But the members of my family love and care for each other very much. We are a close-knit unit. My parents wanted us to be strong and to rely on ourselves. Dad was always there for us, but Mum was the one who drove us to want to do our best. I learned about business and money from her. She would say things like, 'The winner takes all' and, 'Chase your dreams'. Mum knew that losing wasn't fair, but it is life. It's not a good idea to teach children that they can win all the time. In the real world, people struggle.

When I was born, Dad was just starting out in law and money was tight. Mum didn't moan. She had two aims. One was to find useful tasks for me and my sisters. Being idle was frowned on. The other was to find ways to make money. At home, we talked business at dinner. I know some parents keep their work away from the kids. They won't share their problems. But I believe their children never really learn the value of money. Sometimes when they get into the real world they can't cope. We knew what the real world was about. My sister Lindi and I helped Mum with her projects. It was fun. It made for a great sense of teamwork within our family.

I have tried to bring Holly and Sam up in the same way, although I have been lucky to have more money than my parents had. I still think my mum's rules were good and I believe Holly and Sam have learnt the value of money.

Mum made little wooden tissue boxes and wastepaper bins. Her workshop was the garden shed and it was our job to help her. We painted them and stacked them up. Harrods ordered them and sales boomed. She also took in French and German students as paying guests. Hard work and fun were family traits. Mum's sister, Aunt Clare, was keen on black Welsh sheep. She got the idea of starting a company to sell mugs with black sheep on them. Ladies in the village knitted woollies with sheep designs. The company did very well and is still going strong. Years later, when I was running Virgin Records, Aunt Clare phoned me to say that one of her sheep had started singing. I didn't laugh. Her ideas were always clever. Instead, I followed the sheep around with a tape recorder. 'Baa Baa Black Sheep' became a hit. It reached number four in the charts.

*

I went from small cottage industries to setting up Virgin worldwide. The risks became bigger. I learned to be bold in my dealings and ideas. Although I listen with care to everyone, I still rely on myself and make up my own mind. I believe in myself and in my goals. I lost faith in myself only once. By 1986 Virgin was one of Britain's largest private companies, with 4,000 members of staff. Sales had increased by 60 per cent from the year before. I was told I should go public – sell shares in my business. Two of my partners were not keen, because they knew me well. They said I would hate losing control. But the bankers said it was a good idea. It would give me more capital to work with. Other big private companies, like Body Shop and Sock Shop, had gone public. They were doing well.

Pushed hard by the bankers, I made up my mind and launched Virgin on the stock exchange. Around 70,000 people applied for shares by post. Those who had left it too late lined up in the City to buy shares in person. I will never forget walking up the long line of people to thank them for their faith in us. I was very moved when they said things like, 'We're not going on holiday this year, we're putting our savings in Virgin' and, 'We're banking on you, Richard.'

It wasn't long, though, before I came to hate the ways of the City. They weren't for me. Instead of a casual meeting with my business partners on my houseboat to discuss what bands to sign, I had to ask a board of directors. Many of them had no idea at all what the music business was all about. They didn't see how a hit record could make millions overnight. Instead of being able to sign someone who was hot, before our rivals did, I had to wait four weeks for a board meeting. By then, it was too late. Or they'd say things like, 'Sign the Rolling Stones? My wife doesn't like them. Janet Jackson? Who's she?'

I have always made fast decisions and acted on my instinct. Then, I was stifled. Most of all, I no longer felt that I was standing on my own feet. We doubled our profits but Virgin shares started to slip and, for the first time in my life, I was depressed. Then there was a huge stock-market crash. Shares dropped fast. It wasn't my fault, but I felt that I was letting down all the people who had bought Virgin shares. Many were friends and family as well as our staff. But many were like the couple who had given me their life savings. I made up my mind. I would buy all the shares back – at the price everyone had paid for them. I didn't have to pay that much, but I didn't want to let people down. I personally raised the £182 million needed, but it was worth it to keep my good name and my freedom.

The day that Virgin became a private company again was like landing safely after a record attempt in a powerboat or a balloon. I felt nothing but relief. Once again, I was the captain of my ship and master of my fate.

I believe in myself. I believe in the hands that work, in the brains that think, and in the hearts that love.

6. LIVE THE MOMENT

Love Life and Live It To The Full
Enjoy the Moment
Reflect on Your Life
Make Every Second Count
Don't Have Regrets

IT WAS 1997. I was in a round the world hot-air balloon race. Before I left, I wrote a long letter to my children, in case I didn't return. I started the letter by saying, 'Dear Holly and Sam, Life can seem rather unreal at times. Alive and well and loving one day. No longer there the next. As you both know I always had the urge to live life to its full . . .'

I wrote the letter just in case the worst happened. We had taken off at dawn from Marrakech in Morocco. Twelve hours later, it seemed as if we were about to crash in flames into the Atlas Mountains. They say a dying man

58

relives his life in his final seconds. For me, this was not true. All I thought was that, if I escaped with my life, I would never do this again. We fought hard all night to keep the balloon up. By dawn, we were over the desert, where we could come down safely.

As we drifted to earth I sat up on the glass roof of the capsule, watching the beauty of the golden dawn as it broke over the desert. This was a day I never thought I'd see and the rising sun and growing warmth of the day seemed very precious. It made me aware that hard-won things are more valuable than those that come too easily. It reminded me to always enjoy the moment.

I love balloons to such an extent that I have one of my own. It's a small balloon with a wicker basket, like the one in *Around the World in Eighty Days*. I often take family and friends up in it. It is one of the most peaceful places I know. It makes me feel at one with nature. You glide silently along, away from the rest of the world. No one can phone you, no one can stop you. You are free. You look down on towns and fields and people who don't know you're there. You can fly next to a wild swan and hear the

beat of its wings. You can look into the eyes of
an eagle.

Balloons have taught me to reflect more. On
earth, my life is fast and hectic, each moment
full. It can be too busy. We all need our own
space and it's good to pause and do nothing. It
gives us time to think. It recharges our bodies as
well as our minds. I often think of the fishermen I watched that Christmas in Japan. It's in
our nature to strive – so I wondered what they
looked for in life? They seemed content fishing
and feeding their families. They didn't seem
driven to set up fish-canning empires. As far as
I knew, they didn't want to cross the Pacific in
a balloon or climb Mount Everest. They took
each day as it came. They lived in the moment,
and perhaps this is what gave them peace of
mind.

My grandmother lived life to the full. At the age
of 89 she became the oldest person in Britain to
pass the advanced Latin American ballroom-
dancing exam. She was ninety when she
became the oldest person to hit a hole in one at
golf. She never stopped learning. In her mid-90s
she read Stephen Hawking's book, *A Brief*

History of Time, which may make her one of the few people to have read it *all the way through*! Shortly before her death at the age of 99 she went on a cruise around the world. She laughed about it when she was left behind in Jamaica wearing only her swimming costume. Her attitude was that you've only got one go in life, so you should make the most of it.

My parents are getting on and are into their 80s now. Like Granny did, they still hop on and off planes and travel around the world. They have been there at the start and end of all my adventures, cheering me on. They even went looking for me when Per and I were lost in the wilds of the frozen North after our balloon came down in a blizzard in Canada. Their example reminds me to enjoy life.

In 1999, we bought a game reserve in South Africa and built a lovely house. Here we spend time together as a family. In fact, I am so aware of how precious time with them is, I ration myself to only fifteen minutes of business a day when we're together. I don't use modern gadgets like email or mobile phones, but in Africa I did learn to use a satellite phone to keep in touch with the office. Many bosses, who

61

spend all day in their office, are baffled. They ask, 'How can you do it all in just fifteen minutes?'

I say, 'It's easy. *Make every second count.*' That is true in both my business and personal life.

I am able to say that now because I am older and perhaps wiser. It wasn't always the case. My first wife, Kristen, got very irate because I was always on the phone. She said I spent my life working and couldn't draw the line between work and home. She was right. Part of the trouble was that I worked from home. I couldn't resist picking up the phone when it rang, which it did, non-stop. I wished I could just let it ring – but I never knew when it might lead to a nice deal.

Even today, even when I am relaxing, I never stop thinking. My brain is working all the time when I am awake, churning out ideas. Because Virgin is a worldwide company, I find I need to be awake much of the time. One of the things I am very good at is catnapping, catching an hour or two of sleep at a time. Of all the skills I have learned, that one is vital for me. On a bus between Hong Kong and China, for example, when nothing much is going on, I will sleep. I wake refreshed and ready to go for long hours. It's also a very good way of switching off. Winston Churchill and Margaret Thatcher were masters of the catnap and I use their example in my own life.

The Spanish painter, Salvador Dali, had a unique way to savour the moment. When he was bored with life, he would walk in his cliff-top garden. He would pick a perfect peach, warm from the sun, and hold it in his hand to admire its golden skin. He would sniff it. The warm perfume would fill his senses. Then he would take a single bite. His mouth would fill with luscious juice. He would savour it slowly. Then he would spit out the mouthful and throw the peach into the sea below. He said it was a perfect moment and he gained more from that than from eating a basket of peaches.

In a way, regrets are like wanting the peach you have thrown away. It's gone, but you are filled with remorse. You wish you hadn't thrown it away. You want it back. I believe the one thing that helps you capture the moment is to have no regrets. Regrets weigh you down. They hold you back in the past when you should move on.

It's hard to lose out on a business deal, but harder still to suffer from guilt. We all do things we wish we hadn't. Sometimes, they seem like big mistakes, but later, when you look back, they turn out to be small. Regret, which leads to a sense of guilt, can give you sleepless nights. But I believe the past is the past. You can't change it. So, even if sometimes you get things wrong, regrets are wasted and you should move on.

A case of this is when Kristen and I went on holiday to Mexico. She chose a place where there were no phones. No one could get in touch with me. A couple of days before we were due to leave, I tried to hire a boat to go deep-sea fishing. I asked a fisherman if he would take us out the next day. He refused, saying it looked like there might be a storm.

I thought he was holding out for more money. I was eager to go and said I would pay him double. A couple more tourists from the bar said they'd go too, and they also paid double. We were having an exciting day of sport, when I noticed that it was growing dark. The wind rose and it grew cold. It started to rain. They started the engine to head home but the rudder jammed so the boat couldn't steer and went round in circles. The storm grew stronger and the sea was wilder. Huge waves broke over us. People were being sick and the boat was being pounded hard. I was sure she was about to break up and sink.

After an hour, the worst of the storm seemed to have passed. There was calm and a strange light. In fact, we were in the eye of the storm. In the distance I could see a solid black line coming closer across the waves. It was the far wall of the storm and looked alarming. I thought we would all die when it hit us. Kristen was a strong swimmer and she said we should swim for the shore, which was two miles away, and try to beat the storm. Everyone said we were mad, but the fisherman gave us a plank of wood to hold on to and we jumped into the sea. I went from being scared of drowning to the terror of being eaten by sharks. We were swept far down the coast. Two hours later, half frozen, we dragged our way up through the surf, onto the beach. Somehow, we stumbled through mangrove swamps back to the village for help. We found a big boat to go and rescue the fishing boat, but we ran into an even bigger storm and were tossed back to shore. When the storm cleared, they searched for two days, but found nothing.

I could have tried to live with the guilt. Instead, although it was tragic, I realised that I had to apply logic to it. I told myself that the fishermen took the money against their better judgement, but they didn't have to. It was the state of the boat that was the problem, and that wasn't my fault. If a ferry goes down with loss of life, it's not the passengers who are at fault, but the captain or the owners. The story of the lost boat came out when my book was published some years later. The *Daily Mirror* sent a reporter to Mexico to find out what had happened. To my relief, they found the boat and the crew alive and well. The tide and winds had taken them many miles down the coast. It took time to fix their boat and there was no radio and no phones to keep in touch. After we had left for home, they sailed safely into the harbour. I didn't know any of this. I could have spent years living with needless remorse, if I had allowed myself to.

Always living in the future can slow us down as much as always looking behind. Many people are always looking ahead and they never seem content. They look for quick fixes, like winning the lottery. I know that goals are important. Money is important. But the bottom line is money is just a means to an end, not an end in itself. And what is going on now is just as important as what you're planning for the future. So, even though my diary is full for months ahead, I have learned to live for the moment.

7. VALUE FAMILY
AND FRIENDS

Put Family and the Team First
Be Loyal
Face Problems Head On
Money is For Making Things Happen
Pick the Right People and Reward Talent

ONE EVENING, JUST UP the coast from Kingston on the island of Jamaica, I sat on the beach outside a bar, listening to Bob Marley and drinking beer. In the sea, a flock of pelicans were diving after fish. They took turns, one after another, diving into shoals. They seemed to be working as a team so each bird would get a share. Our family was like that, a close-knit team. Virgin is also like a big family. Today, there are some 40,000 members of staff, but each one of those team members counts.

This idea of teamwork came from my child-hood. Mum always tried to find something for us to do. If we tried to escape, she told us we were selfish. One Sunday at church, instead of sitting next to a boy who was staying with us, I slid into the seat next to my best friend, Nik. Mum was hopping mad. A guest was a guest, she said, and guests must be put first. She told Dad to beat me. He didn't. Behind the closed door of his study he clapped his hands to make the right noise and I howled loud enough for Mum to hear. My dad was often out at work and it was Mum who was in control of the children but they were both a big influence, and I continue to get on well with both of them today.

You can be best friends with someone and still not agree with them and, if you are close, you can get through it and remain friends. Nik came to work on *Student* magazine with me. He was good at handling the money side of things. He moved our cash out of the old biscuit tin where we kept it and into a proper bank account. He also helped find us a big house so we could move out of our cramped basement office. I thought things were doing well, so I was shocked when I sat down at my desk one day to find a memo to the staff. The memo said they should sack me as publisher and run *Student* among themselves. Nik had left it there by mistake.

I felt betrayed, but knew I had to turn the crisis around by getting rid of Nik. I asked him to step outside and said, 'Some of the others have come to me and said they don't like what you're planning.' I acted like I knew all about it.

Nik was in shock that he had been caught out. I said, 'We can remain friends, but I think you should go.'

Nik looked sheepish. 'I'm sorry, Ricky,' he said. 'I thought it was for the best.'

He left and we did remain friends. It was the first fight I had ever had with anyone. I was very upset that the fight was with my best friend. But, by facing it head on, I stopped it from getting worse. The lesson I learned was that it's best to bring things out into the open. A dispute with a friend or a colleague can be sorted in a friendly way.

Student continued to grow. We expanded into selling mail-order records. I couldn't do it on my own and offered Nik the chance to come back, and 40 per cent of the new mail-order business if he would return. He bore me no grudge and came back into the fold. Money was always tight in those early days. Nik handled the problem by cutting costs and being nice to debt collectors, who then chased us less often.

He said, 'It's fine to pay bills late, as long as you pay them in the end.'

The mail-order business boomed. But *Student* was taking up too much time, and another problem was cash flow, which was when, if we weren't paid for the magazines before we had to pay our own bills, the flow of cash through the business might dry up. I tried to sell the magazine to IPC, one of the biggest print media groups in the UK at the time. They were eager to have me stay on as editor and asked for my plans. As always, I had plenty of ideas and launched into them. I think the IPC board was stunned when they heard my lavish dreams for the future. I started talking about a cheap student bank, nightclubs and hotels for students. I said we should run a cheap train service and when I mentioned a cheap airline, it was clear that they thought I was a madman.

'We'll let you know,' they said, as they

showed me the door. 'Don't call us, we'll call you.'

That was the end of my big plans for *Student*. Instead, we opened our first record shop. I often wonder what would have happened if IPC had listened to me. Would they, instead of Virgin, have airlines and trains now?

Our next step was to open a studio to make records. I wanted it to be a place where people could come and hang out and have fun. In the early 1970s, recording studios were mostly in London and they were run like an office. They were hostile places for bands to work in. Having to play rock and roll at nine o'clock in the morning was not fun. Also, every band had to drag in their own gear. I wanted to supply everything they needed, from drums to amps. I decided to look for a large country house, where we could all be one big, happy family.

I was excited when I saw an advert for a castle for sale for only £2,000. It was a bargain. I loved the idea of owning a castle. I dreamed of bands like the Beatles had been in the 1960s and the Rolling Stones flocking there to record. Full of high hopes and big plans, I drove to Wales to inspect it. Sadly, the castle was stuck in the middle of a new housing estate. My dreams faded. On the way back to London, I saw another advert for an old manor house near Oxford. It wasn't a castle, but perhaps it would do.

I drove down narrow lanes, off the beaten track. A long drive wound off through trees. The house was at the end. As soon as I saw the lovely, rambling old place, I fell in love with it. Glowing in the evening sun, it stood in its own private park. There was tons of room. The Stones and the Beatles could have a wing each! It was perfect. Excited, I called the estate agent.

'It's £35,000,' he said.

'Will you come down a little?' I asked.

'For a quick sale, you can have it for £30,000. It's a bargain.'

Perhaps it was a bargain – if you had that kind of money. I was thinking more in terms of £5,000. The asking price was so far beyond my reach it didn't seem worthwhile trying to raise it. But I had to try and achieve my dream.

For the first time in my life, I put on a smart suit and polished my old school shoes. I hoped to impress my bank into giving me a loan. Later, they told me that when they saw me in a suit and polished shoes, they knew I was in trouble. I showed them the books for the mail-order business and the shop. To my shock they offered to lend me £20,000. That was a lot of money in 1971. No one had ever lent me that much before. It gave me a real buzz and sense of pride. I felt I had come a long way since the days when I stood in the payphone at school, trying to sell adverts in *Student*. But £20,000 still wasn't enough.

I hoped my family might help. They had always been there for me and I understood then as I still do now how vital that is when you are starting out. My parents had set up small trust funds for my sisters and me. We would have £2,500 each when we were thirty. I went to ask if I could have mine early. They agreed at once. Then Dad said, 'You are still £7,500 short. Where will you get it from?'

'I don't know,' I said.

Dad said, 'Go to lunch with Auntie Joyce. I'll tell her you're coming.'

So I went to lunch with my dear Auntie Joyce. She was the aunt who had bet me ten shillings I wouldn't learn to swim. Dad had called her as he promised. She knew all about my dreams for the Manor. She offered to lend me the money, to be paid back with interest when I could afford it. I started to babble my thanks. She stopped me. 'Look, Ricky, I wouldn't lend you the money if I didn't want to. What's money for, anyway? It's to make things happen. Besides,' she said with a smile, 'I know how you stick at things. You won that ten shillings, fair and square.'

I could still hear her words in my head when I went to pick up the huge key to the Manor. *Money was for making things happen.* I believed it then and I believe it now. I also knew that without my family I would not have been holding that big old iron key in my hand. What I didn't know was that Auntie Joyce didn't have £7,500 to spare. She had such faith in me she had borrowed by taking out a mortgage on her own house.

Thirteen years after buying the Manor, we launched our airline. When we flew to New York, the plane was packed with my family and friends, all the people who counted in my life. As I looked at the proud and happy faces of my family, I knew they had helped make me what I was.

*

I have learned always to reward talent. Even if someone is hired to do one thing, if they have good ideas, or can handle something else, just let them do it. This is why I walk around, asking people's advice in the street, on a plane or on a train. It's true what they say – that the man in the street often has more common sense than many big bosses. Ken Berry is a good example. Ken started in one of our record shops as a clerk. His first job was to check the takings, but before long he was doing many other things. Whenever I wanted to know something, it didn't matter what, I would call Ken. He seemed to know everything about everything. Today, people turn to Google or Yahoo. We just asked Ken.

Two of the best things about him were that he could get on with people, and that he didn't have an ego. We found he was good at dealing with anyone from the top stars to their lawyers. Soon we had him working on the contracts. It was obvious that his talents were wasted as a clerk and he joined our small team in running Virgin. He became Chief Executive Officer of Virgin Music and, a lot later on, of EMI.

As usual, I didn't always follow Ken's advice. Once, when we had grown too fast and were running out of cash, I called a crisis meeting. At the time, our top seller was Mike Oldfield's *Tubular Bells*. Its massive sales funded everything. But our contract with Mike had expired and he was pushing for more money to renew it. I was very frank with him. I told him that the whole of Virgin Music was making less money than he was on his own.

'Why?' he asked.

I explained that we had many bands that didn't make any money at all.

'So I finance it all?' he said.

I nodded. 'Yes, pretty much.' I thought he would be pleased to learn how many bands he was helping to support.

But he looked peeved. 'I'm not giving my money away for you to blow it on a load of rubbish,' he said. 'You can afford to pay me more.'

At the crisis meeting, I said all our eggs were in one basket. We needed to sign more bands and singers. We needed more hits in order to spread the risk and increase the size of the company.

Ken Berry had been doing his sums. 'It's clear to me that we need to get rid of all our bands, apart from Mike Oldfield,' he said.

I knew we could jog along and make money with Mike Oldfield, but I was worried we would stay the same small company. And if his records stopped selling, we would sink almost without a trace. I told Ken that we needed to find a new big band – fast!

To save money, we cut back to the bone. We sold our cars. We closed the swimming pool at the Manor. We didn't pay ourselves. Those were easy savings. The hard ones were dropping some artists and losing staff. But we had to cut right back to survive. We came through at last when we signed the Sex Pistols. They were the start of punk – which was the new big thing.

On a funny note, when we dropped Dave Bedford, who wrote great music, he wrote me a very nice letter, saying he understood. It was pages long, all very friendly and polite. He also wrote to Mike Oldfield, calling me all the vile names under the sun. It was a pity for him that he then put the letters in the wrong envelopes!

*

People have asked me how I can take so much time off to go on adventures around the world. My answer is that when you pick the right people, you can leave them to it. You know that things will run smoothly if you're not there. In 1987, I was in the middle of a boardroom battle to buy EMI, when I had to dash off. I had agreed to fly a balloon across the Atlantic with Per, and the weather was right. If we delayed, we could miss the moment. I went, knowing that I had the right people to talk the deal through. However, with the very real risk that I might die, the talks were put on ice until I returned – if I returned.

The hurricane in October of that year blew away all our dreams of owning EMI. The stock market crashed and our shares dropped in value. The banks didn't have faith that things would go up again and wouldn't lend us the money. In the end, I forgot about our takeover bid. Strangely, during the 'dirty tricks affair' with British Airways, when I was struggling to keep the airline afloat, I had to sell Virgin Music to EMI for half a billion pounds. It was one of the saddest days of my life – but in business you have to make some very hard choices. If the airline had gone under, hundreds of people would have lost their jobs. That half a billion made us safe for a very long time and gave me the cash to start up new businesses. And Virgin Music was also safe. The team all survived, which was the main thing.

If anyone asks me what I believe in above all else, I would say my family. I firmly believe in the family. I know that sometimes they split up, and I have been through some of that myself. And I know that some people don't have anyone. But close friends can be like a family. We all need a strong support network. Even though I was taught to stand on my own feet, without my loyal family and friends I would be lost.

8. HAVE RESPECT

Be Polite and Respectful
Do the Right Thing
Keep Your Good Name
Be Fair in All Your Dealings

IN THE EARLY DAYS of Virgin Music, I talked to some Japanese businessmen. They were very polite to a young man in sweater and jeans who had no money. They taught me how important it was to always keep eyes and ears open and to be polite. They say that you never know who might hear or see you. People talk. Gossip has a habit of getting back to those you gossip about.

I have come across this myself. One time I had to go to a meeting. I was late. I grabbed some papers and jumped into a taxi. On the way, the driver got very chatty. He said, 'Oi! I know you. You're that Dick Branson. You've got a record label.'

'Yes, that's right,' I said.

'Well, ain't it my lucky day. Fancy having Mr Branson in my cab.'

I hoped he might shut up so I could read my papers for the meeting, but he went on. He told me he might be a cabby by day, but he was also a drummer in a band. He asked if I'd like to hear his demo tape. My heart sank. People were always playing tapes to me in the hopes they would be discovered.

But I didn't want to be rude. 'That would be lovely,' I said.

'No, you look tired. Tell you what, my mum lives around the corner. She'd love to meet you. Let's drop in and have a quick cup of tea.'

'No, I'm late–' I started to say.

'I insist, guv. A cup of tea's what you need.'

'Thank you,' I said, weakly.

Just as we reached the house, the driver put on his tape. I heard the words over the speakers: 'I can feel it, coming in the air tonight ...' He jumped out of the front seat and held the door open for me. The cab driver was Phil Collins, laughing like mad.

When I made *The Rebel Billionaire*, I copied the idea from Phil. I made myself look like an old cabby and drove the young contestants to the manor house, where we would be filming. I had my ears peeled and listened to what they said in the back. I also noted how they treated an old man who couldn't lift heavy cases. I learned a lot about them from that, much to their dismay.

Respect is about how to treat everyone, not just those you want to impress.

The Japanese can wait 200 years for a long-term goal for their company. They don't look for the quick buck. They want slow, solid growth. One time, I was looking for a partner to take a stake in Virgin Music. We talked to many Americans. They wanted to invest, but they also wanted to be hands-on, which means closely involved, in the running of the company. We had our own way of working, so we wanted a silent partner. We knew a partner that was too hands-on could cause conflict. I remembered the businessmen from Japan who had treated me so kindly a few years before, so we turned to the East. I asked the Japanese businessman who came to see me how he saw us working together.

'Mr Branson,' he asked gently, 'would you

prefer an American wife or a Japanese wife? American wives are very difficult – lots of divorce and alimony. Japanese wives are very good and quiet.'

Good and quiet didn't mean weak. It sounded perfect – and we went with his company.

One of the best lessons I ever learned was when I did something illegal. I got caught and paid for it. At the time, I thought I was being a bit of a long-haired, hippie pirate. It even seemed a game. I was being bold – but I was also being foolish. Some risks just aren't worth it.

During the 1970s we were all a bit hippie and thought it was fun to break the law. The mood was very much 'us and them'. Pirate radio stations were blasting the airwaves from offshore. People were doing drugs by the wagonload. My scam seemed a neat little trick. It started by chance in the spring of 1971. Virgin was known for selling cool, cut-price records and we had a large order from Belgium. If you exported records to Belgium, you didn't have to pay tax on them, so I bought these tax-free records direct from the record companies and hired a van to take them across the Channel on the ferry. My plan was to land in France and drive on to Belgium. I didn't know that in France, you had to pay tax.

At Dover the customs people stamped my papers with the number of records I had. When I arrived in France, I was asked for proof that I wasn't going to sell the records in France. I showed my order from Belgium and said I was just passing through France, but it did no good. The French said I had 'bonded stock' and had to pay tax.

We argued, but since I didn't want to pay the tax, I had to return by ferry to Dover with all the records still in the van. I was angry that I had wasted my time and lost a good order. But on the drive back to London it dawned on me that I now had a vanload of tax-free records. I even had a customs stamp to prove it. I thought I could still sell them by mail order or in the Virgin shops and make about £5,000 extra profit.

It was against the law, but I just thought I was bending the rules a bit. After all, I had started out trying to do the right thing. At the time, Virgin owed the bank £15,000. It seemed as if luck, or fate, was helping us out. I had always got away with breaking rules and thought this was no different. I would have got away with it if I hadn't been greedy. Instead of just selling the one vanload, I made a total of four trips to France, pretending each time that the records were for export, and turned right around again. The last time, I didn't even bother getting on the ferry. After I got my stamp from customs, I just drove in a circle in the port at Dover, in one gate and out the other, and headed home. I am sure that if I hadn't been stopped I might have carried on. It was so easy. Only it wasn't as easy as I thought. I was being watched.

I got a tip-off that we were about to be raided. We had one night to get rid of all the tax-free stock. We cleared out our warehouse, but we thought that customs wouldn't bother with our shops. When the customs men burst into the warehouse, I hid a grin while I watched them search for the illegal records. I didn't know that they were also raiding the shops at the same time. It was a huge shock when I was thrown into prison.

I couldn't believe it. I thought that only criminals were arrested. And then it slowly dawned on me that I wasn't a hippie pirate. This wasn't a game. And I *was* a criminal. My headmaster's words came back to me. When I left school, aged sixteen, he had said, 'Branson, I predict that you will either go to prison or become a millionaire.'

I wasn't a millionaire – but I was in prison. My parents had always drummed into me that all we had in life was our good name. You could be rich, but if people didn't trust you, it counted for nothing. I lay on a bare plastic mattress with just an old blanket and vowed that I would never do anything like this again. I would spend the rest of my life doing the right thing.

In the morning, Mum came to the court to support me. I had no money for a lawyer and applied for legal aid. The judge told me if I asked for legal aid I wouldn't get bail. He set bail at a whopping £30,000. I didn't have that kind of money. I had the Manor, but it was still mortgaged. Mum put up her home as bail money instead. Her trust in me was almost more than I could bear. She looked at me across the court and we both started to cry.

I will always remember her words on the train

back to London. 'I know you've learned a lesson, Ricky. Don't cry over spilled milk. We've got to get on and deal with this head on.'

Instead of going to court, the customs service agreed to settle the case. They made me pay a fine equal to three times my illegal profit. It came to a massive £45,000. They said I could pay it back at the rate of £15,000 a year. I wasn't angry. I had shown the law no respect and deserved to pay. Not doing anything illegal has been one of my watchwords since then.

My way of restoring my own respect was to pay back every penny without moaning. In fact, I gained. My goal became to make a lot of money, but to do it legally. We worked like crazy, opening new Virgin Records shops and thinking up good ideas to expand.

Ever since then, when I am asked how far I am prepared to go in achieving my aims, my answer is the same. I make it a priority not to break the law and I check all the time that I'm not. Your reputation is everything.

If you're starting in business and ask me if I have a lesson for you, I'd say, 'Be fair in all your dealings. Don't cheat – but aim to win.' This rule should extend to your private life.

My motto is, 'Never do anything if it means you can't sleep at night.' It's a good rule to follow.

9. DO SOME GOOD

Change the World, Even If In a Small Way
Make a Difference and Help Others
Do No Harm
Always Think What You Can Do To Help

I WAS BROUGHT UP to think we could all change the world. I believed that it was our duty to help others and to do good when we could. I'm sure my headmaster was stunned when I wrote a long report about how he could run the school better. I ended grandly with the words, 'I would be very interested in your views on this, and any money saved could be put towards my next plan . . .'

He didn't laugh, or even cane me for my cheek. He handed back my report and said dryly, 'Very good, Branson. Put it in the school magazine.'

Instead, I left school and started my own

magazine. I wanted to use it as a platform to change things. When my sister Lindi and I were trying to sell copies of *Student* in the street, a tramp asked me for money. I didn't have a penny, but I was so fired up to do good, I tore off my clothes and gave them to him. I had to spend the rest of the day wrapped in a blanket, but I felt quite noble.

One of the ways we tried to help people was by starting a students' advice centre. They could ask about anything, from flats to grants, but mostly they asked for advice about sex. At the time, there was nowhere else to go for the kind of advice we offered. The centre did so well that, 35 years later, it's still going strong.

I spent the next few years building up Virgin. Making money was nice, but it wasn't my main aim in life. I enjoy hard work. The man who started IKEA divides his day into ten-minute sections. He says, 'Ten minutes, once gone, are gone for good. Divide your life into ten-minute units, and don't waste even a minute.' You don't have to fill your time rushing about in order to use your time wisely, though. Bill Gates – the world's top charity donor – said his staff could spend two hours gazing into space, as long as their minds were working, and Albert Einstein came up with the theory of relativity in his head without paper or pen. He only wrote it down later. To be honest, I work out all my best ideas in my head too. And because I don't use my hands for my work, perhaps that is why I enjoy taking time off for hard physical tasks, like crossing the Atlantic in a boat.

It's said that money is the root of all evil. It doesn't have to be. Money can be used for good. The biggest charities in the world were started by rich men and women, but some were begun with next to nothing. Harvard, the wealthiest college in America, is a charitable trust. It started with a few books and just $350. IKEA started in a garden shed. Its parent company is a charitable trust. The man who dreamed up the Big Mac started life selling paper cups. He was someone else who didn't believe in wasting time. 'If you have time to lean, you have time to clean,' he always told his staff. Perhaps he was in a hurry because he didn't get the idea for McDonald's until he was aged 52. His company now gives $50 million a year to charity.

So money can be a force for good. But you don't need to be rich to do good. Children used to collect silver paper and empty cola tins to raise money for good causes. Today, they go on charity runs or donate to Live Aid. There are many ways of helping others. One very simple way is to do no harm and that costs nothing at all.

When I turned forty, I was at an all-time low. We were battling with British Airways for space in the skies. We had been voted Best Business Class Airline of the year, but it was a constant fight to find enough money to keep going. It was only Virgin Music's string of hit records that was keeping us afloat. Simon, who ran Virgin Music, seemed to be losing interest in it – mostly because he thought the airline would bankrupt us. I sat down and looked back at my life. I asked myself if I should do something new, if I should have a complete change. I had never been a big reader, but I liked the idea of having more time to read.

I said to Joan, 'I think I might go to college and do a degree in history.'

'You just want to chase pretty girls,' was her blunt reply.

Was she right? Was I facing a midlife crisis?

Perhaps. So, instead of thinking what I could do for myself, I wondered if I could do more for others. I thought I might look into politics. I could use my business skills to do some good on major issues, such as fighting cigarette companies. I could fund a cure for cancer, look into health care, or help homeless people. There were many things I could do that would make me feel useful. I have gone on to follow this path in the rest of my life.

I believe we should all assess our lives from time to time. Have we reached our goals? Are there things we can weed out that we don't need? I'm not talking about throwing away old shoes or broken chairs. I mean we need to lose our bad habits or lazy ways that hold us back and clutter our minds.

My cousin, Sir Peter Scott, ran a famous wetlands bird reserve. When I told him I wanted a lake at my home in Oxford to attract wild birds, he came and gave me advice. I dug it out and built several islands for birds to nest on. Swans, ducks, geese and herons flew in from all over the place. It's a very peaceful spot, somewhere I can think things through. Normally, I like to be in a crowd of people or with my family, but sometimes, you need space. I like to walk around the lake on my own, just thinking.

When I was fighting to survive with the airline, it was one of the few times when I felt totally lost. As I walked around the lake I had some big decisions to make. When I had told the bank that Virgin Music was worth at least half a billion pounds, they had wanted me to sell it to cover their loans to the airline. I had two choices: to close the airline or sell the record company. The problem was that I thought I could keep both. I just needed the bank to keep its nerve. It seemed to me that, as long as they knew how valuable the music side was, their debt was safe. But banks don't like risk and they said that if I didn't sell it they would withdraw my loans. I wasn't sure what to do. I loved Virgin Music and knew that as a company it would continue to grow. We had just signed the Rolling Stones as well, and I felt as if I would be letting them and all our other musicians down. I wasn't sure what to do on that rainy day as I walked around the lake.

In the middle of this worrying time, in August 1990, Iraq invaded Kuwait. I heard on the news that 150,000 refugees had crossed into

Jordan. I was friends with King Hussein and Queen Noor of Jordan. The queen was a beautiful woman, a highly trained Arab-American architect who had met her husband when she was working for Jordan airlines. We had a lot of things in common. She had seen me on TV during my balloon flight around the world and phoned to ask if I would teach the royal family to fly in a balloon.

I had shipped a balloon to Jordan and met the royal family. They were all as lovely as she was and the children were polite and friendly. I had a great time, flying over the capital, looking down on ancient, red-tiled roofs. When the people below realised that their king and queen were floating along in a wicker basket above their heads, they ran along, looking up and cheering. It was a difficult time for the king. There had been many attempts on his life and armed bodyguards were always around him, except they didn't know how to protect him when he was up in the sky without them. But for King Hussein it was a welcome moment of complete freedom.

When Saddam Hussein invaded Kuwait, I watched the thousands of refugees flooding over the border on the television. I phoned King Hussein and Queen Noor and asked if I could help. I wanted to make a difference. The queen said she would see what needed to be done and would get back to me. Later that day she phoned to ask if I could get them some blankets. The desert was very hot during the day and very cold at night. She said blankets could be rigged up to give shade during the day and at night people could roll up in them to keep warm.

'A few very young children have already died,' Queen Noor said.

'How many blankets do you need?' I asked.

She said they needed 100,000. 'We've got only two or three days before hundreds start to die. It's urgent, Richard.'

Virgin airline staff got to work, phoning around. In two days one of our jumbo jets was on its way to Jordan with 40,000 blankets, tons of rice and medical supplies. We returned with British people who had been stranded in Jordan. As soon as I returned to Britain, I was told that the head of British Airways was hopping mad. He said they should have been asked. It was pointed out to him that I had offered and he hadn't. In fact, he had apparently refused to let BA help in international crises, even when approached by Christian Aid. So, at once, he found a load of blankets and rushed them to Jordan. I was pleased that our example had partly pushed him into helping.

When I heard that our supplies had not reached all the refugees, I flew to Jordan and again stayed with the king and queen in the royal palace. I argued with a minister who I knew had blocked things from moving and got him to send the supplies to the refugee camps. I also had long talks with King Hussein about Saddam. The king wanted Jordan to remain neutral in the conflict that by then seemed likely. His country was in a very weak position and he also saw both sides of the picture. He hoped things could be sorted out through talks – but he was worried that the West might go to war to protect the oilfields in Kuwait. He knew there was very little time.

A few days later I was watching the news in London, when I saw Saddam on the TV. He had taken British hostages and was using them as a human shield. I thought about what I could do to help. I was one of the very few Western people who had direct access to King Hussein. He in turn was one of the very few people that Saddam trusted. We could cut out all the angry people in the middle and perhaps get somewhere before there was a war. I got the idea that perhaps Saddam would exchange the hostages for medical supplies and that perhaps King Hussein could talk to Saddam and put my suggestion to him. I called Queen Noor and asked if she could help with my plan.

'Come on out and stay with us, Richard. You can discuss it with the king yourself,' she said.

In Jordan yet again, I spent three days talking to King Hussein. He agreed that something must be done quickly before things got worse. I sat down and with a lot of care wrote a very polite letter by hand to Saddam. I asked if he would release all the foreigners who were trapped in Iraq. To show goodwill I would fly in medical supplies that Iraq was short of. I signed it, 'Yours respectfully, Richard Branson.'

After dinner that night, the king took my letter to his study and translated it into Arabic. He also wrote his own personal cover letter to

Saddam and sent it by special courier to Iraq. I could do no more and flew home.

Two nights later, I heard from King Hussein. It was very good news. Saddam said that he would release the sick hostages and the women and children, but he wanted someone of stature to fly to Iraq and ask him in person, on TV. I phoned Sir Edward Heath, the former prime minister. We got on well because of our mutual interest in boats. Very bravely, he agreed to go at once. The plan was that he would first fly to Jordan to stay with the royal family. From there, he would get safe passage to Iraq.

A day later, King Hussein phoned me. 'I have good news for you, sir. You can set off for Iraq. I have Saddam's word that you will be safe.'

I had one major worry before I set off. In spite of King Hussein's promise, many expected Saddam to take me and Edward Heath hostage and impound the plane. Because of the risk, we had no insurance. If Saddam did seize the plane, we would go bust. I was risking everything on this venture – but too many people depended on me. There was no backing out.

When we left Iraq with the hostages and Edward Heath safely on board, we were so relieved we partied all the way back. But one person wasn't happy. The boss of BA said, 'Who the hell does Richard Branson think he is – part of the bloody Foreign Office?'

Afterwards, I wrote in my diary, 'What are the motives for doing such things? A month ago, I was at an all-time low. I seemed to have run out of a purpose in my life. I'd proved myself in many areas. I'd just turned forty. I was seeking a new challenge . . .'

When I re-read what I had written, I realised that as a *businessman* I could do a great deal of good. The rescue mission to Iraq had proved it. As a businessman, I meet incredible people like Nelson Mandela, world leaders like the Russian premier, and people of vast wealth like Bill Gates and Microsoft's lesser-known co-founder Paul Allen. In fact, people in business and the very wealthy are in a unique position. They can connect with everyone, whether high or low, in any country, through a network of good will.

I believe they can use that power wisely, for the good of the world – exactly as I said in my first ever *Student* column. My daughter Holly, who is a medical student, is interested in the sexual issues facing young people in the UK. We have come full circle from where I started out in the world, as she volunteers when she can at Virgin Unite and at the Student Help Centre, where students can contact us at Portobello Road in West London if they need counselling.

My original love, music, is also a strong force for good. You only have to look at Live Aid and Live 8 and the incredible work that people like Peter Gabriel, Bono and Bob Geldof do in raising money for famine relief and other disasters in the Third World to see that. Princess Diana did so much for charity when she was alive, and I was pleased to be able to help her with that in some small way. So I was very proud when I persuaded Elton John to sing 'Candle in the Wind' at her funeral. The record sold 33 million copies worldwide and made £20 million. This was all given to charity, exactly as Diana would have wished.

In 2004 I brought myself closer to my vision of helping more people by setting up Virgin Unite. It is intended as a way of getting all the Virgin staff around the world to work together to help with tough social problems. I hope we can continue to make a difference.

EPILOGUE

I HAVE ALWAYS LIVED my life by thriving on chances and adventure. The motive that drives me has always been to set myself challenges and try to achieve them. Every lesson I have learned has been as a direct result of these tests. They include:

- Just do it
- Think yes, not no
- Challenge yourself
- Have goals
- Have fun
- Make a difference
- Stand on your own feet
- Be loyal
- Live life to the full

The best time of the day for me is evening, at Necker, seated around a big, happy table, with my family and friends having fun. This paradise island combines many of my dreams and aims in life. When Joan and I first found the island, buying it became a goal. Raising the money and building a house on it, then getting water in, were huge tests to be passed. I never once said, 'can't'. I went for it, and we did it. Today, it's a place where my family and friends and I have a lot of fun. It's where I relax and think – and where some of my best ideas come out of the blue. I have to keep an open mind to see their virtue.

I started to play tennis more on Necker. It's good to concentrate on the game and think of nothing else. Having learned to focus without my mind wandering and, after many years of avoiding books, I started reading more about nine years ago. I have always read, but not heavy books, but I was surprised and pleased at how quickly I got going. I speed read but, thanks to my early problems at school, absorb it all. I don't allow myself to trip over slow or tricky words, but get the meaning from the flow and sense of the section. Now that I have started, reading has become a great pleasure. I like history books best – which has led to my interest in archaeology. At the moment, I am funding a dive off the coast of Egypt to survey the ancient city of Alexandria. My favourite books are *Stalingrad* by Antony Beevor and *Wild Swans* by Jung Chang.

But I still can't use a laptop. People have given me a Blackberry and mobile phones, but I have always written everything down in school notebooks. It started when I found reading and writing hard at school and, to make up for that, built up a very good long-term memory. Now, I jot down key words in my notebooks and later, if I need to, I find a note and I can recall entire conversations. This has stood me in very good stead more than once when I have needed to prove something. But it's not just conversations – I also jot down my own thoughts. Anything I see and hear can spark an idea in me. I note it down at once and often look back through old notebooks to gain fresh ideas or to see what I might have missed. I would advise young people starting out in life to keep a notebook with them. It's a good habit to get into.

I still believe in all the tasks my mother set us, but have applied them to a lesser degree with my own children, Holly and Sam. They live in the modern world, but like me they were brought up to challenge themselves. I encouraged them but never pushed them. Joan is a very down-to-earth Scottish woman. She made sure that we were always around other family members. We live a very stable, normal life and as a result, Holly and Sam are very well balanced.

All the things in this book are my lessons and my goals in life, the things I believe in. But they are not unique to me. Everyone needs to keep learning. Everyone needs goals. Each and every one of my lessons can be applied to all of us. Whatever we want to be, whatever we want to do, we *can* do it. Go ahead, take that first step – just do it.

INDEX

RANDOM READS

BRILLIANT BOOKS TO INFORM AND INSPIRE

Other books in the Random Read series

RANDOM **READS**

BRILLIANT BOOKS TO INFORM AND INSPIRE

Bloody Valentine

James Patterson

Arrow

This year Valentine's Day isn't for romance.
It's for murder.

Mega-rich restaurant owner Jack Barnes and his second wife Zee are very much in love. However, their plans for Valentine's Day are about to be torn apart by the most violent murder. Who is the strange figure plotting this sick crime? Who hates Jack that much? There are plenty of suspects living in Jack's fancy block of flats. Is it one of them, or could it be the work of an outsider with a twisted mind? One thing's for sure, the police have got their work cut out solving this bloody mess.

This gory murder mystery will make you feel weak at the knees.

RANDOM **READS**

BRILLIANT BOOKS TO INFORM AND INSPIRE

Desert Claw

Damien Lewis

Arrow

In present day Iraq thieves roam the streets. People are being killed in broad daylight. Security is non-existent. And now, terrorists have seized a Van Gogh painting worth £25 million from one of Saddam's palaces. They are offering it to the highest bidder . . .

Mick Kilbride and his buddy 'East End' Eddie are ex-SAS soldiers. The British Government doesn't want to pay the ransom money to the terrorists. Instead, it hires Mick and his team of ex-Special Forces to get the painting back and leave no man alive. Their mission takes them into a dark and violent world where all is not as it seems. And if Mick and Eddie are going to stay alive, they're going to have to stay one step ahead of the enemy . . . and their betrayers.

RANDOM **READS**

BRILLIANT BOOKS TO INFORM AND INSPIRE

Last Night Another Soldier

Andy McNab

Corgi

A short, sharp shot of danger.

Afghanistan, 2009. A rifle section is halfway through their six-month tour of duty in Helmand Province. Sixteen men have already been killed. Forty-seven others have been wounded and flown back home.

The last three months have been tough and it shows. Their kit is in a bad way. They are in a bad way. Young men with tans, scruffy beards, peeling noses and lips burnt raw by the Afghan sun. Despite the hardships, they are enjoying their time out here learning how to fight the Taliban. The lads are on their way to becoming the best soldiers in the Army.

Last Night, Another Soldier is the story of four of the young men in this rifle section, partly told from the point of view of eighteen-year-old squaddie, David 'Briggsy' Briggs.

RANDOM **READS**

BRILLIANT BOOKS TO INFORM AND INSPIRE

Strangers on the 16:02

Priya Basil

Black Swan

A very ordinary train journey goes horribly wrong.

It's a hot, crowded train. Helen Summer is on her way to see her sister Jill to tell her an awful secret. Another passenger, Kerm, is on his way back from his grandfather's funeral.

They are strangers, jammed against each other in a crowded carriage. Noisy school kids fill the train – and three of them are about to cause a whole heap of trouble. In the chaos, Helen and Kerm are thrown together in a way they never expected.

Catching a train? Read *Strangers on the 16:02* and you'll never feel the same way about your fellow passengers again.

LET US ENTERTAIN YOU!

RANDOM **READS** are brilliant short books by bestselling writers and famous people. Some are stories, some are real-life experiences, others offer advice on business or life in general.

Whether you read a lot or a little, or would simply like to read more, there will be Random Reads to inform and inspire you.

RANDOM **READS**

BRILLIANT BOOKS TO INFORM AND INSPIRE

The Thief

Ruth Rendell

Arrow

What you do in childhood may come back to haunt you.

Stealing things from people who had upset her was something Polly did quite a lot.

There was her Aunt Pauline; a girl at school; a boyfriend who left her. And there was the man on the plane . . .

Humiliated and scared by a total stranger Polly does what she always does. She steals something. But she never could have imagined that her desire for revenge would have such terrifying results.